LEARN TO RE

LEARN TO
CO

Vowel Reference Card
Phonics

Written by Carolyn Torres
Illustrated by Nicholas Torres

Collection 11: This is a collection of five stories that builds on the previous collections by adding the Phonetic Vowel Reference Card words. In this collection, instead of only short vowel sounds and the long vowel sounds formed when a "silent e" is added to the end of the word, all the rest of the vowel sounds on the Vowel Reference Card will be used. All five stories are written with the *Dolch phonetic Sight Words and other Phonetic Vowel Reference Card Words. Each story will have a list of vocabulary words at the beginning as well as questions to answer at the end.

*The 315 Dolch Sight Vocabulary list is taken from the Picture Word Cards and Popper Words Set 1 (included in item #0-07-609422-7), plus Popper Words Set 2 (#0-07-602539-X) published by SRA (1-888-SRA-4543 or SRAonline.com).

NEXT BOOK

Collection 12: This is a collection of five more Phonetic Vowel Reference Card stories. Each story will have a list of vocabulary words at the beginning as well as questions to answer at the end.

DEDICATION

These books were created for children to help them learn how to read by using phonics skills systematically. These books are dedicated to parents, giving them an early literacy practical guide with tools.

ACKNOWLEDGMENTS

These books were created for _Schuler Phonics CORE (Second Part)_, authored by Mary M. Schuler. This collection includes Companion Stories #48-52.

It is highly recommended that BEFORE reading this book, your child/student should study the following sections in _Schuler Phonics CORE (Second Part)_ Vowel Reference Card by Mary M. Schuler:

1. Single Consonants with Short Vowels
2. The FLOSS and CK Rule
3. Adding s and 's to nouns and verbs
4. Blends with Short Vowels
5. Digraphs with Short Vowels
6. Adding es to nouns ending s, x, z, ch, or sh
7. The Silent e Rule.
8. Compound Words and
9. Vowel Reference Card

www.parentreadingcoach.org
FOR TRAINING VIDEOS

Schuler Phonics and Companion Books
WHERE "Sound it out" really works!

But to help it work, note the following:

Any word _italicized_/_underlined_ in these stories should NOT be sounded out --- because sounding out just won't work on those words! (The words, "The" and "the" will not be italicized/underlined even though considered "non-phonetic"; there are just too many of them, and they really are not a problem!)

IMPORTANT for Collection 11: One sound but more than one letter (ea, au, aw, al, all, ai, ay, ee, igh, oa, ow, ew, oo, ar, or, er, ir, ur, oy, oi, ou) will be typed in **bold** in the words in these stories to help parents/students spot those vowel reference card sounds.

All of these words can be sounded out using the Vowel Reference Card!

Joseph's Vowel Reference Card

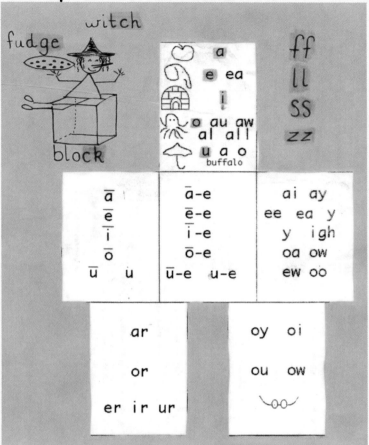

NOTE: Do you see the Silent e sounds right in the middle of the Vowel Reference Card? What do the a, e, i, o, and u say there?

NOTE: Now, single a, e, i, o, u do not just say the short vowel sound but also could say the long vowel sound. The letters a and o, also, have a third sound. Can you find all those sounds for a, e, i, o, and u?

NOTE: ea, ow, oo and y each have two sounds. Can you find those two sounds for each one?

It is highly recommended that BEFORE reading this book, you, parents, should watch the training video, Deep Dive, on www.parentreadingcoach.org, while viewing Joseph's Reading Review Column on page ix).

It is highly recommended that BEFORE reading this book, you, parents should practice with your child the word lists provided by having your child:

1) circle the vowel sound from the vowel reference card;

2) say the vowel sound; and

3) read the word.

Repeat until mastery is reached.

Example

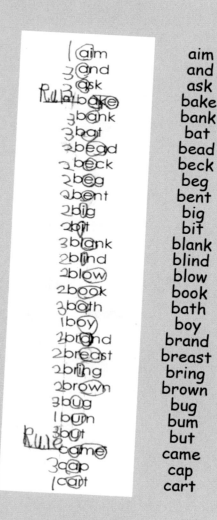

aim
and
ask
bake
bank
bat
bead
beck
beg
bent
big
bit
blank
blind
blow
book
bath
boy
brand
breast
bring
brown
bug
bum
but
came
cap
cart

For the stories in this collection your child should learn the following underlined/italicized words and parts of words by sight (Do NOT sound out --- It doesn't work!):

are
cake/_walk_
come
comes
could
_do_
does
done
door
duck/_walk_
eye
eyes
farm/_house_
four
full
give
gives

have
hen/_house_
horse
horses
horses'
house
in/_to_
know
laugh
live (short i)
lives (short i)
_of_
once
once-a-year
one
on/_to_
pull

pulls
put
puts
said
shall
shoe
shoe/horn
shoes
should
sleep/_walk_
some
some/one
some/time
some/times
the
their
there

they
_to_
_to_/day
two
u/_pon_
walk
want
wants
wash
were
where
who
work
would
you
your
your/self

All the other words can be sounded out as they are based on short vowel and single consonant, blend, and digraph words, silent e rule, compounds, plus Vowel Reference Cards words.

<u>IMPORTANT NOTE FOR PARENTS/TEACHERS</u>:

<u>A</u> or <u>a</u> should NOT be pronounced as long a (/ā/ as in the word say) in the phrase/sentence such as, "<u>A</u> Real Girl," or "Doc wants to make <u>a</u> doll into <u>a</u> real girl." Instead, <u>A</u> or <u>a</u> should be pronounced as a short u (/ŭ/ as in umbrella /ŭ/ or up /ŭ/).

The e in the words <u>The</u> or <u>the</u> should NOT be pronounced as long e (/ē/ as in the word bee) in the phrase/sentence such as "<u>The</u> Tall Oak Tree, or "<u>The</u> owl hoots at the moon at night." Instead the e in <u>The</u> or <u>the</u> should be pronounced as a short u (/ŭ/ as in umbrella /ŭ/ or up /ŭ/).

CONTENTS

STORY 1: PHONICS

The Tall Oak Tree

IMPORTANT: Before studying this vocabulary with your child and before having your child read the story note the following:

This is the third Companion Book to use the Vowel Reference Card words. Up to this point only the non-phonetic Dolch words have been marked in the stories (<u>*underlined and italicized*</u>). Now, however, the Vowel Reference Card teams will be marked in **bold** to help you, parents, help your children spot those vowel teams and <u>**refer them to the Vowel Reference Card**</u> to figure out their sound(s) and therefore be able to read the words.

(Note: The Vowel Reference Card is in the very back of this book!!!)

The single letters a, e, i, o, u, and now also y will not be marked at all as usual. However, parents, for example, if your child sees a single letter o in a word, like in dog, or go, or from, your child needs to be made aware that there are three possible sounds for that letter o (<u>**refer them to the Vowel Reference Card**</u>), not just octopus /ŏ/ as it has been up to this point! This is true for the single letters a (three possible sounds), e (two possible sounds), i (two possible sounds), u (three possible sounds), and y (two possible sounds). Silent e sounds still will not be marked in any way.

COMPANION STORY 48: PHONICS

Non-phonetic Dolch sight words:
(*underlined /italicized as usual*)

<u>*are*</u>	<u>*know*</u>	<u>*there*</u>
<u>*come*</u>	<u>*live*</u> (short i)	<u>*they*</u>
<u>*comes*</u>	<u>*lives*</u> (short i)	<u>*to*</u>
<u>*do*</u>	<u>*of*</u>	<u>*two*</u>
<u>*does*</u>	<u>*once*</u>	<u>*want*</u>
<u>*eye*</u>	<u>*once-a-year*</u>	<u>*wants*</u>
<u>*eyes*</u>	<u>*one*</u>	<u>*were*</u>
<u>*full*</u>	<u>*said*</u>	<u>*you*</u>
<u>*have*</u>	the	
in/<u>*to*</u>	<u>*their*</u>	

Phonetic vocabulary to practice:
Note the Vowel Reference Card teams in **bold**.

a	by	**d**own/strok
a/cross	call	e
all	**calls**	**dream**
and	can	duck
a/round	caw	**eat**
a/sleep	caws	**far**
at	chick	**far-off**
a/**way**	chicks	**far-out**
back	claw	fast
be	claws	**feast**
beak	cool	feed
beaks	crane	finch
bend	cross	find
best	crow	fish
big	cry	**flew**
bird	dawn	**flight**
birds	day	flock
black	day/light	flown
branch	day/time	fly
branches	dead	food
br**ight**	did	**for**
br**ow**n	dive	from
bug	dives	gave
bugs	don't	gold
bunch	dove	g**oo**d
but	down	grab

4

grabs	I	moon/light
grasp	in	my
grass	is	near
gray	it	need
green	its	needs
greet	join	nest
greets	joins	new
ground	joy	night
had	keen	noon
harm	keep	not
has	kept	now
hawk	leaf	oak
hawk's	left	off
he	light	old
hear	like	on
hears	likes	or
her	long	out
her/self	look	owl
hide	look/out	part
high	lot	quack
him	lots	red
him/self	loud	rest
his	low	right
hole	may	round
home	may/be	saw
hoot	me	say
hoots	meal	scold
how	mole	scolds
hurt	moon	scoop

see
sees
self
sharp
she
sky
sleep
small
smart
snack
snake
so
soon
south
speed
spot
squeak
star
stars
start
starts
straw
stream

strike
stroke
stuff
sun
sun/down
sun/light
sun/up
swipe
take
tall
tell
that
them
then
thing
things
three
time
too
took
tool
top
tree

trunk
twig
twigs
up
use
wake
wakes
was
way
well
what
when
which
white
will
wing
wings
wise
with
wood
year

The **tall oak tree** had big, long, _full_, green branches, which _were_ home **for** lots _of_ birds.

A wise, br**own owl** did _live_ **high** up in a ro**un**d hole n**ea**r the top _of_ the **tree** trunk.

You will not hear the **owl** when the sun is **out**, when _there_ is **light all** around. The **owl** _comes_ **out** with the **stars**, at sundown. The **owl** hoots at the moon at **night**. He can **look far-out**, **far-off**, and **see small** bugs fly by in the moonlight. The top _of_ the **tree** is his lookout!

The **owl** is **smart** and has **keen** <u>eyes</u>. When he **sees** a mole on the **gro**und, he dives **down** fast, with his best **speed**, and grabs it **for** a m**ea**l.

When a n**ew** day **starts**, at sunup, with the d**aylight**, at d**awn**, the black cr**ow** wakes up.

The black cr**ow** likes <u>to</u> fly ar**ound** in the d**ay**time <u>to</u> look **for** br**ight** things.

The cr**ow** **saw**, with his **keen** <u>eyes</u>, the sun**light** strike a t**ool** on the **gro**und.

"I _want_ that white **tool**," _said_ the black **crow** _to_ himself.

The **crow** flew **right** down _to_ grasp the bri**gh**t, white **tool** on the gr**ou**nd, t**oo**k it _to_ his straw nest in the **tall oak tree**, and kept it. The **crow caws** and scolds at **all** the small birds _to_ tell them _to_ keep away from his old and **new** stuff.

The red and black **hawk** with a big nest in the **tall oak tree** can fly and dive well.

One _of_ the **hawk's** chicks gave a **lou**d cry.

Two _of_ the **hawk's** chicks gave a **lou**d cry.

Three _of_ the **hawk's** chicks gave a **lou**d cry.

"Squeak, squeak, squeak!"

With a big **downstroke** _of_ its **wings**, the **hawk** dove **down** in_to_ the **tall**, green grass _to_ swipe a snake with **her** claws.

She **flew** the de**a**d snake back *to* her nest *to* **feed** her chicks. The chicks **feast** on the de**a**d snake with *their* sharp beaks.

At n**oo**n, the gr**ay**, white, red, and black crane left its flock *to* find f**oo**d. It **flew** across the sky *to* the **tall oak tree**. The crane has a long beak with which *to* **scoop** fish **out** *of* the stream. The gr**ay**, white, red, and black crane will rest at the top *of* the **oak tree** and **eat** its fish.

The **oak** tr**ee** is not home **f**or the crane, but the tr**ee** is a c**oo**l spot <u>to</u> rest and **ea**t fish.

"That was a g**oo**d fish," <u>said</u> the **g**ra**y**, white, red, and black crane <u>to</u> herself.

"Now, how _do_ I find my flock? I will call _to_ them, but _have_ _they_ flown too fast and too far? _Are_ _they_ too far away _to_ hear me?"

The gray, white, red, and black crane calls _to_ her flock. The flock calls back. The crane greets her flock and then joins them on _their_ flight home.

The brown and green wood duck _wants_ _to_ fly south. It has flown all day now with its flock and needs _to_ sleep for the night. It will hide, asleep, by the tall oak tree in back _of_ a big, green leaf.

Will it dream? I don't (_do_ not) _know_. **May**be it will. **S**oon it will wake and **say,** "Quack, Quack, Quack." When it h**ears** the rest _of_ its flock, it will fly **sou**th with them on _their_ _once_-a-y**ear** flight.

The red and gold finch is a **small** bird that _lives_ by a bunch _of_ twigs n**ear** the bend in the long branch at the **low** part _of_ the **tall oa**k **tree**. The **small** finch has _to_ hide from the big b**ir**ds n**ear** the top _of_ the **tree** so _they_ will not **hurt or** harm **her**. The finch will **feast** on bugs **for** a snack.

What a **joy** <u>to</u> <u>live</u> in, on, near, **or** by the big **oak tree!**

Questions to check:

1. When will you hear the wise, brown owl?
   a. when it is light out
   b. at sunup
   c. at night, in the moonlight

2. When does the black crow wake up?
   a. at night
   b. in the moonlight
   c. at daylight, at sunup

3. Which bird did swipe a snake to feed her chicks?
   a. the black crow
   b. the red hawk
   c. the wise, brown owl

4. Which two birds use the tall oak tree to rest, but the oak tree is not their home?
   a. the black crow and the black and red hawk
   b. the gray crane and the brown and green wood duck
   c. the red finch and the wise, brown owl

5. What small bird hides down low from the birds near the top of the tree?
   a. the red and gold finch
   b. the black crow
   c. the wise, brown owl

STORY 2: PHONICS

A Real Girl

IMPORTANT: Before studying this vocabulary with your child and before having your child read the story note the following:

This is the third Companion Book to use the Vowel Reference Card words. Up to this point only the non-phonetic Dolch words have been marked in the stories (_underlined and italicized_). Now, however, the Vowel Reference Card teams will be marked in **bold** to help you, parents, help your children spot those vowel teams and **refer them to the Vowel Reference Card** to figure out their sound(s) and therefore be able to read the words.

(Note: The Vowel Reference Card is in the very back of this book!!!)

The single letters a, e, i, o, u, and now also y will not be marked at all as usual. However, parents, for example, if your child sees a single letter o in a word, like in dog, or go, or from, your child needs to be made aware that there are three possible sounds for that letter o (**refer them to the Vowel Reference Card**), not just octopus /ŏ/ as it has been up to this point! This is true for the single letters a (three possible sounds), e (two possible sounds), i (two possible sounds), u (three possible sounds), and y (two possible sounds). Silent e sounds still will not be marked in any way.

COMPANION STORY 49: PHONICS

Non-phonetic Dolch sight words:
(_underlined /italicized as usual_)

are	_of_	_to_
_do_	_once_	_to_/day
does	_one_	_two_
done	_put_	_walk_
eye	_puts_	_want_
eyes	_said_	_wants_
full	_shall_	_were_
give	_shoe_	_where_
gives	_shoes_	_who_
have	_some_	_work_
in/_to_	_some/one_	_would_
know	the	_you_
laugh	_there_	_your_

Phonetic vocabulary to practice:
Note the Vowel Reference Card teams in **bold**.

a	am	a/r**ou**nd
add	and	at
adds	a/p**ar**t	b**all**
a/live (long i)	**ar**m	be
all	**ar**ms	b**ear**

bear/cat	cheeks	fit
best	chest	five
big	child	foot
birth	clay	for
birth/day	cross	fore
black	dark	fore/arm
blond	day	fore/arms
bloom	dead	for/get
blow	deep	form
blue	did	forms
bone	Doc	found
bones	doll	from
born	doll's	gave
both	dress	get
brain	each	gets
breath	ear	girl
bright	ears	glad
bring	end	glue
brown	fall	gold
brush	feed	good
brushes	feeds	good/will
but	feet	got
can	fell	gray
can/not	find	grow
case	finds	hair
cat	fine	hand
check	fire	hands
checks	fires	hard
cheek	first	has

hat	like	out
he	lip	paint
head	lips	paint/brush
help	live (long i)	paint/brushes
her	long	paints
high	lot	palm
hold	lots	pant
hole	lung	pants
holes	lungs	part
hop	made	parts
hope	make	pill
hug	makes	pills
hugs	man	pink
I	may	plus
in	may/be	point
in/side	more	real
is	most	red
IS	mouth	rib
it	must	ribs
IT	my	right
joy	neck	round
jump	need	run
just	next	scarf
keep	nose	see
left	not	sees
leg	now	she
legs	off	shine
let	on	short
light	or	show

side	such	turn
skill	sun	up
skin	sun/dress	use
skirt	sun/light	uses
skull	take	was
small	tall	wave
smart	teeth	well
smile	ten	what
snow	that	when
snow/ball	then	which
snow/man	thing	white
so	things	will
soon	think	wind
speak	this	wish
spot	throat	wish/bone
spread	time	with
stand	TIME	with/out
stands	toe	wound
still	toes	wow
stripe	top	zap
stripes	toy	
strong	try	

Doc _wants_ _to_ make a doll in_to_ a
real girl.

First, Doc has _to_ make the doll. Without a doll, _there_ cannot be a real girl!

Doc has lots _of_ _work_ _to_ _do_ on the skull.

Doc forms a ball out _of_ clay. What a fine round head the doll will _have_! Doc makes holes for _eyes_ and for a mouth.

Doc fires the clay _to_ make it hard. She sees that the skin _of_ the skull is white.

Then, Doc _gives_ the doll _two_ ears, _two_ blue _eyes_, a nose, and a mouth with teeth for a big smile, which will show joy.

The doll will need a brain _to_ help her _to_ think and speak.

Doc did not forget the doll's brain. When she made the skull out _of_ the ball _of_ clay and made holes for the _eyes_ and mouth, she made a spot _to put_ a big, smart brain inside the doll's skull! She did not fire the brain! The brain was _put_ in when Doc _put_ in the doll's _eyes_.

She uses strong glue so the **ears**, _eye_s, nose, m**ou**th, and t**ee**th will not **fall** off. Doc gets h**er** paints and _some_ small, fine paintbrushes. The doll's lips _are_ s**oo**n br**igh**t red. The doll's cheeks _are_ pink.

Doc finds _some_ blond hair, _some_ gold hair, _some_ red hair, _some_ gray hair, _some_ black hair, _some_ pink hair, and _some_ brown hair. The doll's head is soon _full_ _of_ long, gold hair, which will blow in the wind and shine with the sunlight.

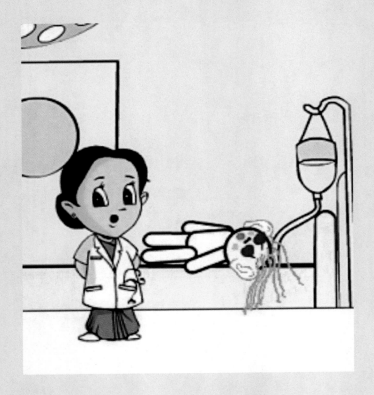

Next _to_ the doll's neck, with the throat inside, is the chest with lots _of_ ribs. The doll will _have_ ten plus _two_ ribs on **her right** side and ten plus _two_ ribs on her left side, just like a **real girl**. The lungs inside the chest, inside the ribs, will let the doll take a d**ee**p br**ea**th.

There are lots _of_ things inside the doll _you_ cannot **see**. _You_ cannot **see** the brain _once_ Doc _puts_ it inside the doll. _You_ cannot **see** the ribs. _You_ cannot **see** the lungs. But the brain, the ribs, and the lungs _are there_ inside the doll.

Doc then adds long **arms** and for**arms**, which _are_ the best _to give_ strong hugs. Hugs bring **joy**. The for**arms** _have_ hands at the end with big **palms**, which can wave. Waves spr**ea**d **goo**dwill.

Doc then adds _two_ **tall** legs with strong **feet**. **Each foot** has five toes so the doll can _walk_ and run with skill. With**out** toes, it _would_ be hard **for** the doll _to_ _walk_ **or** run well.

IT IS TIME! The doll has **all her parts**. The doll is _done_! Now Doc must try _to_ turn the doll in_to_ a real girl. Doc will use her wishbone _to_ make the doll in_to_ a real girl.

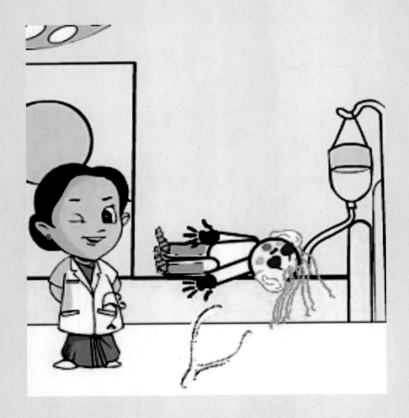

Where did Doc get such a big wishbone? Doc got the wishbone from the bones _of_ a big, big, big bearcat, which _was_ dead and fell apart. The bones _were_ not good _to_ keep, but the wishbone still was. _Who_ gave her the wishbone? Doc did _know_ _someone_ _who_ found that big, big, big, dead bearcat. He gave Doc the wishbone.

Doc finds a hat, a scarf, a top, a short skirt, a dress, _some_ pants, and _some_ _shoes_ _to_ fit the doll. The doll now has on a dark blue dress and _some_ white _shoes_ with stripes. _Does_ she _have_ the scarf wound around her neck?

"Get _your_ wishbone, Doc.

Hold it up **high** with both _of your_ hands!

Think. Wish h**ar**d.

Po**in**t the wishbone at the doll."

Maybe this will _work_! I hope so!

ZAP _to_ the skull! ZAP _to_ the brain! ZAP _to_ the hair. ZAP _to_ the **eyes**, **ears**, nose, and mouth. ZAP _to_ the chest and lungs. ZAP _to_ the **arms** and legs and hands and toes.

Wow! It did _work_!

Wow! The doll is **now** a **r**eal **girl**.

Wow! The **r**eal **girl now** has blond **h**air and br**own** skin.

Wow! The **r**eal **girl now** has black _eye_s.

What a zap!

Doc checks the **real girl**. Doc **fee**ds the **real girl** _some_ pills.

<u>One</u> more ZAP, just in case!

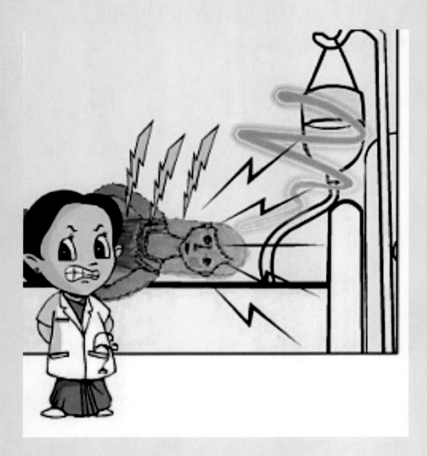

The doll stands up. She has on a dark blue sundress and _some_ white _shoe_s with stripes. She _does_ not _have_ a scarf wound around her neck. Doc must not _have_ _put_ that scarf on the doll!

Doc _said_, "_To_day _you were_ born. _To_day is _your_ birthday. _To_day is the birthday _of_ my real girl made from a doll!"

"_You are_ but a child, but _you shall_ bl**oo**m and g**row**." I am so glad _you are_ alive."

The real girl did _laugh_ and jump with joy!

Doc and the real girl _were_ both _full of_ joy.

Questions to check:

1. Doc wants to make a _____ into a _____.
   a. toy cat, real cat
   b. doll, real girl
   c. snowball, real snowman

2. The skull has two ____, two blue ____, a _____, and a _____ with lips and teeth.
   a. eyes, ears, nose, mouth
   b. ears, eyes, mouth, nose
   c. ears, eyes, nose, mouth

3. What will let the doll take a deep breath?
   a. the lungs
   b. the eyes
   c. the ears

4. The long arms give ____. The forearms with hands can ____. The _____ can run.
   a. joy, hop, ears
   b. joy, jump, eyes
   c. joy, wave, feet

5. What two things did Doc do to turn the doll into a real girl?
   a. Doc gave the doll a hug and said, "ZAP!"
   b. Doc did wave at the doll and said, "ZAP!"
   c. Doc did use her wishbone and said, "ZAP!"

STORY 3: PHONICS

The Farm

IMPORTANT: Before studying this vocabulary with your child and before having your child read the story note the following:

This is the third Companion Book to use the Vowel Reference Card words. Up to this point only the non-phonetic Dolch words have been marked in the stories (_underlined and italicized_). Now, however, the Vowel Reference Card teams will be marked in **bold** to help you, parents, help your children spot those vowel teams and **refer them to the Vowel Reference Card** to figure out their sound(s) and therefore be able to read the words.

(Note: The Vowel Reference Card is in the very back of this book!!!)

The single letters a, e, i, o, u, and now also y will not be marked at all as usual. However, parents, for example, if your child sees a single letter o in a word, like in dog, or go, or from, your child needs to be made aware that there are three possible sounds for that letter o (**refer them to the Vowel Reference Card**), not just octopus /ŏ/ as it has been up to this point! This is true for the single letters a (three possible sounds), e (two possible sounds), i (two possible sounds), u (three possible sounds), and y (two possible sounds). Silent e sounds still will not be marked in any way.

COMPANION STORY 50: PHONICS

Non-phonetic Dolch sight words:
(_underlined /italicized as usual_)

are	_horse_	sleep/_walk_
cake/_walk_	_horses_	the
come	_house_	_their_
_do_	in/_to_	_there_
does	_know_	_they_
door	_once_	_to_
duck/_walk_	_pull_	_walk_
farm/_house_	_pulls_	_were_
four	_put_	_who_
full	_shoe_	_work_
have	_shoe_/horn	
hen/_house_	_shoes_	

Phonetic vocabulary to practice:
Note the Vowel Reference Card teams in **bold**.

a	boxes	**cows**
all	**brown**	crash
and	bump	did
a/**round**	**burst**	dog
as	but	don't
a/sleep	by	**dream**
at	cake	drink
a/**way**	**care**	duck
back	c**art**	ducks
b**ark**	cat	dusk
b**arks**	ch**ase**	**each**
b**arn**	chick	egg
b**arn**/yard	chicks	eggs
b**athe**	**cloud**	**fall**
b**ear**	**clouds**	**farm**
b**ears**	**cloud**/**burst**	**farm**/yard
bed	cluck	fast
big	colt	**fee**d
black	**cool**	**figh**t
box	**cow**	**foal**

for	hurt	name
from	if	names
front	in	neat
gate	in/side	no
get	is	not
glad	its	off
good	jaw	on
got	jaws	or
grass	jog	out
green	jump	out/side
ground	keep	own
growl	keeps	past
growls	lay	peck
hand	left	peep
hand/cart	let	pen
has	like	pet
hen	lot	pets
hens	lots	pig
hide	loud	pigs
his	man	pig/pen
horn	meet	play
horns	more	pup
how	mud	Pup

rain
ran
rams
right
roll
round
rounds
run
runs
sad
safe
same
seed
shake
shakes
sheep
sheep/dog
side
sky

sleep
sleeps
small
smart
sneak
snort
sound
splash
steer
still
straw
stream
sun
swine
take
takes
that
them
these

this
time
took
trail
up
was
way
what
when
while
white
wife
wild
win
with
with/in
won
yard

A man and his wife **own** a **farm**. *They* *have* a **farm**_house_ with a big yard r**igh**t **out**side the front _door_ _of_ the **farm**_house_. This **farmyard** has a gate. Off _to_ the r**igh**t and _to_ the left _of_ the **farmyard**, **out**side the gate, _there_ is a **b**arn, a **b**arnyard, a hen_house_, a pigpen, and a **sheep** pen. In back _of_ the **farm**_house_, _there_ is lots _of_ green grass and a **stream**.

There _are_ lots _of_ pets on the farm.

The cat, the pup, the hens, the chicks, the ducks, the wild swine (pigs), the **c**ows, the **shee**pdog, the **shee**p, the **f**o**al**, the colt, the **stee**r, the rams, and more _are_ all pets _to_ the man and his wife.

All the pets _have_ names.

The cat and the pup **slee**p inside the big **f**arm_house_ in _their_ **ow**n small _house_ in the same bed.

In the big **yard**, the **farmyard**, **out**side the front _door_ _of_ the farm_house_, _there_ _are_ lots more pets.

The pup and the cat _come_ **out** in_to_ the **farm**yard _to_ **play** with the hens and _their_ chicks. The chicks **pee**p and **pee**p and **pee**p. The hens and _their_ chicks peck at the **see**d on the gr**ou**nd. The pup and the cat jog ar**ou**nd by the hens and the chicks.

The pup _pull_s a duck ar**ou**nd the **farm**yard in a **cart**.

"Don't (_do_ not) let the duck **fall out**, Pup!"

The cat, the pup, the hens, _their_ chicks, and the ducks _know_ how _to_ get past the gate.

Once, in a dr**ea**m, the pup did
sleep_walk_ **ou**tside the gate. The
pup, in the dr**ea**m, got up and
while still asl**ee**p, _put_ on its duck
_shoe_s with a _shoe_horn and did a
duck_walk_ with _four_ ducks ar**ou**nd
a cake_walk_. The pup won the cake
in its dr**ea**m!

The hens _were_ in the hen_house_. _They_ did cluck and **lay** _their_ white eggs in the st**raw** in _their_ boxes in the hen_house_. These hens t**oo**k _their_ chicks **out** _to_ fe**ed** when the chicks did **p**ee**p**.

The pigpen is _full_ _of_ br**ow**n mud.
The wild swine bathe and jump
and roll in the mud. When a duck
and the cat **sneak** **ou**t _of_ the ya**r**d
past the gate, the wild swine in
the pigpen like _to_ splash mud at
them. Was that a wild swine in
the sky?

There is a big barn on the farm. The man and his wife keep _horses_ and cows in the barn. The foal is black and the colt is brown. The foal and colt like _to_ chase the steer around the barn. The steer run and hide by the stream.

The cows drink from the stream and sleep on the green grass when the sun is out or when _there are_ clouds, but no rain. If _there_ is a cloudburst, the cows run for the barn.

The sheepdog, at dusk, rounds up the sheep, runs them on the trail back _to_ the sheep pen, and keeps them safe from the bears. The sheepdog growls and barks at the bears _to_ keep them away.

The sheepdog takes good care _of_ the sheep.

The rams _are_ loud as _they_ bump and crash _their_ horns outside the barn. What a sound! The ground shakes each time _their_ horns meet. _Do_ _they_ fight _to_ win? No. _They_ like _to_ _work_ and play this way. _Does_ that hurt _their_ jaws?

What a neat, cool, farm with lots _of_ smart, glad, not sad, pets.

Questions to check:

1. Who sleeps in the same bed inside the farmhouse?
   a. the cat and the pup
   b. the hens and the ducks
   c. the wild swine and the sheep

2. What do all the pets have?
   a. a bed within the farmhouse
   b. a handcart
   c. names

3. What do the hens do when they lay eggs?
   a. They fall out of the cart.
   b. They cluck.
   c. They run fast.

4. Who do the wild swine like to splash mud at?
   a. the horses and cows
   b. the cat and a duck
   c. the sheepdog

5. The sheepdog _____ the sheep and takes good _____ of them.
   a. shakes, care
   b. rounds up, care
   c. pulls, care

STORY 4: PHONICS

The Seeds

IMPORTANT: Before studying this vocabulary with your child and before having your child read the story note the following:

This is the third Companion Book to use the Vowel Reference Card words. Up to this point only the non-phonetic Dolch words have been marked in the stories (_underlined and italicized_). Now, however, the Vowel Reference Card teams will be marked in **bold** to help you, parents, help your children spot those vowel teams and **refer them to the Vowel Reference Card** to figure out their sound(s) and therefore be able to read the words.

(Note: The Vowel Reference Card is in the very back of this book!!!)

The single letters a, e, i, o, u, and now also y will not be marked at all as usual. However, parents, for example, if your child sees a single letter o in a word, like in dog, or go, or from, your child needs to be made aware that there are three possible sounds for that letter o (**refer them to the Vowel Reference Card**), not just octopus /ŏ/ as it has been up to this point!   This is true for the single letters a (three possible sounds), e (two possible sounds), i (two possible sounds), u (three possible sounds), and y (two possible sounds). Silent e sounds still will not be marked in any way.

COMPANION STORY 51: PHONICS

Non-phonetic Dolch sight words:
(_underlined /italicized as usual_)

are	_pull_	_two_
could	_put_	_u/pon_
_do_	_said_	_want_
done	_some_	_wash_
horse	_some_/time	_were_
horses'	_some_/times	_who_
in/_to_	the	_would_
know	_their_	_you_
_of_	_there_	_your_
once	_they_	_your_/self
one	_to_	

Phonetic vocabulary to practice:
Note the Vowel Reference Card teams in **bold**.

a	clouds	**forth**
all	cob	**found**
am	cobs	fresh
and	**cook**	from
a/round	corn	fry
at	corn/cob	fry/pan
a/way	corn/cobs	glove
back	cut	gloves
bad	dad	gold
barn	Dad	**good**
black	dad's	got
boy	dark	grass
boy's	day	green
bug	days	grew
bugs	did	ground
burn	dig	grow
burst	dirt	grown
but	don't	hard
by	dry	hay
can	dug	he
care	dust	heat
case	each	help
check	feast	here
cloud	find	high
cloud/burst	fire	him
cloud/bursts	for	him/self

his	me	row
hit	might	rows
hole	moon	saw
holes	moon/light	saw/dust
hope	more	seed
hose	my	seeds
hot	my/self	self
husk	near	shine
husks	no	short
I	not	shuck
if	now	small
in	off	so
is	oil	soft
it	on	soil
just	or	son
keep	out	Son
kill	pan	soon
kind	plant	sprout
lawn	plants	stall
left	pop	stalls
let	pop/corn	store
lid	proud	store/room
light	rain	stove
long	ran	straw
look	rich	strong
looks	room	stuff
lot	root	sun
lots	roots	sun/shine
low	round	tall

taste	times	weed
than	told	weeds
that	took	week
them	tool	weeks
then	tools	well
these	top	went
thick	twist	what
think	up	when
those	us	white
three	was	will
tight	way	with
time	we	yum

Once *upon* a time, a small boy
went in*to* his dad's barn.

The small boy did look here and
there. He did look high and low.
He did dig in stuff in the straw,
in the sawdust, and in the hay.
He dug here and *there* in the
tools, around the *horses*' stalls,
and in the storeroom.

He found *some* seeds!
He found *some* seeds!!
He found *some* seeds!!!

The **small** b**oy** ran <u>to</u> his dad.
"Dad, I <u>want</u> <u>to</u> plant these s**ee**ds
in the gr**ou**nd, in the black, d**ar**k,
rich d**ir**t n**ea**r <u>your</u> plants."

Dad <u>said</u>, "What kind <u>of</u> plants
<u>are</u> <u>they</u>?"

"I don't (<u>do</u> not) <u>know</u>," <u>said</u> the
small b**oy**.

Dad **looks** at the **see**ds the b**oy fou**nd.

"Those **see**ds will <u>*work*</u>. <u>*They*</u> will g**row** well in the black, d**ark**, rich s**oi**l in back <u>*of*</u> my plants. <u>*They* *are*</u> popc**orn** see**ds**."

The small boy dug _one_ hole in the ground. He _put_ in _two_ seeds, just in case _one_ _of_ the seeds was bad. He dug _one_ more hole in the dirt and _put_ in _two_ more seeds. Then he dug and dug and dug in more soil. He _put_ _two_ seeds in each hole. _Some_times he _put_ in three seeds, just in case!

He _put_ dirt on top _of_ each _of_ the _two_ or three seeds. He did plant _two_ rows _of_ popcorn, and then he ran out _of_ seeds.

"I am prou**d** _of_ _you_, Son," _said_ his dad _to_ him.

A cloudburst, a hard rain, for a short time _would_ not _wash_ away the seeds. A cloudburst, a hard rain, for a long time _would_ _wash_ away the seeds. _There_ _were_ no cloudbursts for a long time!

With _some_ days _of_ clouds and soft rain and lots _of_ days _of_ sunshine, the popcorn plants soon did sprout and burst up from the ground. It took _two_ weeks.

The **boy took** care _of_ his popcorn plants. If more than _one_ plant gr**ew** up in **ea**ch hole, the sm**all** b**oy** left just _one_ plant so it _could_ gr**ow** strong! Dad told the sm**all** b**oy** _to do_ that! If _there_ was no rain, the sm**all** b**oy** got the hose _to_ help the plants. The sm**all** b**oy** did think _of_ that **all** by himself!

<u>*Some*</u> bad, green plants grew with the popcorn plants. Those bad, green plants <u>*were*</u> weeds. The boy did <u>*pull*</u> up the weeds from <u>*their*</u> roots. He did <u>*pull*</u> up the roots from **all** the thick, green weeds that grew so <u>*they*</u> <u>*would*</u> not kill the good popcorn plants.

When the popcorn plants _were_ **all tall, all** grown, and _done_ (Dad did check!), the **boy** and his dad did _pull_ the corncobs off the plants. _They_ did shuck the green husks off the gold popcorn **see**ds.

"Now let us dry them. Then the popcorn seeds will just twist off the cobs," _said_ the boy's dad.

"I can twist the gold popcorn seeds away from the corncobs myself," _said_ the small boy. "It is not hard! I will not cut myself, but gloves might help me not _to_ cut myself!"

Dad did not help the boy _to_ twist the popcorn seeds away from the corncobs, but he did find him _some_ gloves.

"_To_ cook," Dad _said_, "We will heat the popcorn seeds in hot oil in a frypan on the stove."

"_Do_ not burn _your_self, Son. Keep the lid on tight! _Pull_ the pan back and forth. The popcorn seeds will pop from the heat and hit the lid."

"Pop! Pop! Pop!" went the popcorn seeds.

The b**oy** and his dad ate **all** _of_ the hot, fresh, white pop**c**orn in the pan. It did taste **s**o g**oo**d!

The **small** b**oy** and his dad _said_, "Yum! Yum! Yum!" lots _of_ times.

What a f**eas**t!

Questions to check:

1. What did the small boy hope to find in the barn?
   a. dirt
   b. seeds
   c. holes
2. What kind of seeds did he find?
   a. popcorn seeds
   b. grass seeds for the lawn
   c. hay seeds
3. Once the seeds did sprout, the small boy left ____ plant in each hole.
   a. three
   b. two
   c. one
4. The seeds need __ and __ to sprout and grow.
   a. weeds, bugs
   b. fire, moonlight
   c. rain, sunshine
5. Who did twist the gold popcorn seeds away from the corncobs?
   a. the small boy and his dad
   b. his dad
   c. the small boy
6. "We will heat the ____ in __ in a pan on the __.
   a. popcorn, hot oil, stove
   b. hay, fire, grass
   c. plants, hot oil, stove

STORY 5: PHONICS

What is in the Lake?

IMPORTANT: Before studying this vocabulary with your child and before having your child read the story note the following:

This is the third Companion Book to use the Vowel Reference Card words. Up to this point only the non-phonetic Dolch words have been marked in the stories (_underlined and italicized_). Now, however, the Vowel Reference Card teams will be marked in **bold** to help you, parents, help your children spot those vowel teams and **refer them to the Vowel Reference Card** to figure out their sound(s) and therefore be able to read the words.

(Note: The Vowel Reference Card is in the very back of this book!!!)

The single letters a, e, i, o, u, and now also y will not be marked at all as usual. However, parents, for example, if your child sees a single letter o in a word, like in dog, or go, or from, your child needs to be made aware that there are three possible sounds for that letter o (**refer them to the Vowel Reference Card**), not just octopus /ŏ/ as it has been up to this point!   This is true for the single letters a (three possible sounds), e (two possible sounds), i (two possible sounds), u (three possible sounds), and y (two possible sounds). Silent e sounds still will not be marked in any way.

COMPANION STORY 52: PHONICS

Non-phonetic Dolch sight words:
(_underlined /italicized as usual_)

are	_of_	_their_
come	_one_	_there_
could	on/_to_	_they_
_do_	_put_	_to_
does	_said_	_walk_
four	_should_	_where_
full	_some_	_who_
have	_some_/time	_you_
in/_to_	_some_/times	_your_
live (short i)	the	

Phonetic vocabulary to practice:
Note the Vowel Reference Card teams in **bold**.

a	can	drift
all	care	dry
a/long	cat	**eat**
an	cat/fish	**eats**
and	clam	egg
a/round	clams	eggs
as	clam's	**far**
at	**claw**	far-a/way
a/way	claws	fat
back	**clean**	**feast**
be	**cleans**	**feet**
beach	clown	fire
best	clown/fish	fire/fly
big	count	fish
black	crab	**float**
black/fish	crabs	fly
bleed	**crawl**	foot
blood	**creep**	**for**
blue	cut	frog
blue-green	dead	frogs
brown	**deep**	from
bug	**dirt**	get
bugs	dive	gets
bump	don't	glove
bumps	down	gloves
but	down/stream	go

gold	lot	rock
gold/fish	lots	rocks
grab	mass	room
green	masses	round
grow	may	run
hand	may/be	salt
hard	might	sand
has	most	scale
help	my	scales
high	my/self	sea
hurt	near	self
hurts	need	shark
I	needs	sharks
if	no	shell
in	not	shrimp
is	old	skin
it	on	slime
its	or	small
it/self	out	smooth
jump	pad	snail
krill	pick	snails
lake	pinch	snap
lakes	pinches	so
land	plant	spot
lay	plants	stream
let	pole	swim
like	poles	tad
likes	red	tad/pole
long	red/fish	tad/poles

take	toad	wear
taste	toads	whale
that	too	what
them	trout	when
then	try	which
thing	up	will
things	wave	with
think	waves	yes
those	way	

The blue-green lake is _full_ _of_ lots _of_ things.

Are _there_ fish in the lake? Yes, _there_ _are_ lots _of_ fish that swim in the lake.

The trout likes _to_ jump and snap at bugs. _Some_times it gets _to_ eat them! Fat bugs taste the best!

The goldfish likes _to_ float with the waves and then drift along, downstream, _to_ a far-away spot.

The catfish cleans up the lake as it eats clams, plants, bugs, small fish, snails and _some_times dead things down deep. A catfish has slime on itself, on its skin and scales, but _does_ not eat the slime, I don't (_do_ not) think.

Is _there_ a shark in the lake? No, _there_ is not a shark in the lake. The lake _does_ not _have_ salt. Sharks swim in the sea _where_ _there_ is salt.

Are *there* crabs in the lake? Yes, *there* *are* crabs in the lake. Most crabs *walk* **or** run on the sand **or** d**i**rt **or** rocks *of* the lake; *they* *do* not swim. *They* like *to* cr**ee**p and crawl **ou**t *of* the lake on*to* the b**ea**ch.

Crabs like _to_ pinch things with _their_ claws. Crabs like _to_ pinch _you_ when _you_ try _to_ pick them up.

When a crab pinches, a **small** crab _does_ not pinch **too** hard, but a big crab pinches hard, hard, hard, and it hurts a lot. _You_ might bleed and _have_ blood from a deep cut on _your_ hand.

Take care not _to_ let a big crab pinch _you_ when _you_ pick _one_ up. **May**be wear gloves!

If a big crab pinches _you_, _put_ it back in_to_ the lake, and it will let go _of_ _you_.

Is _there_ a whale in the lake? No, the lake is **too small** for a whale. A whale is big. A whale ne**e**ds lots _of_ r**oo**m _to_ swim ar**ou**nd in and then dive d**ee**p. A whale likes _to_ f**ea**st on shrimp and krill that _live_ in the s**ea**.

Are _there_ frogs in the lake? Yes, _there_ _are_ frogs _who_ jump up h**igh** _to_ grab a firefly **or** land on a pad. Frogs **lay** masses _of_ eggs in the lake. Tadpoles will _come_ from those eggs. Sm**all** frogs will g**row** from those tadpoles. Frogs _are_ gr**ee**n and sm**oo**th. The gr**ee**n, sm**oo**th frog **eats** lots _of_ bugs.

Are _there_ clams in the lake? Yes, _some_ clams _live_ in lakes. Clams _do_ not _have_ **arms** _to_ help them _to_ swim, but _some_times the clam's **foo**t will help it swim. _You_ _could_ cut _your_ **foo**t and bl**ee**d if _you_ _walk_ on an old clam shell. _You_ _should_ swim in the lake, not _walk_, so _you_ don't (_do_ not) h**ur**t _your_ f**ee**t.

Is _there_ a **toa**d in the lake? No, **toa**ds like dry land that is n**ear** a lake **or** a stream. **Toa**ds _are_ bro**w**n and _full_ _of_ bumps.

Can _you_ **c**oun**t** **all** the things I _said_ m**igh**t be in the lake? I _come_ up with _four_ myself (fish, ..., clams). What _do_ _you_ _come_ up with?

Questions to check:

1. What three fish were in the lake?
   a. clownfish, blackfish, redfish
   b. shark, whale, clownfish
   c. trout, goldfish, catfish
2. What three things were not in the lake?
   a. the whale, the shark, and toads
   b. the crabs, the fish, the frog
   c. the clownfish, the frog, clams
3. What likes to creep and crawl out of the lake and pinch with its claws?
   a. clams
   b. crabs
   c. frogs
4. Which likes dry land the best, a toad or a frog?
   a. the toad
   b. the frog
5. Which is brown and full of bumps?
   a. the toad
   b. the frog

Glossary

Dolch/Sight Words: Words your child should <u>first</u> sound out, using phonics, and then master by sight, so sounding out is no longer necessary.

Phonics: A practice of sounding out words.

Consonants: Sounds, phonemes, which are blocked by the teeth, tongue, and/or lips. Sometimes it is just easier to think of consonants as all the letters that are not vowels: b, c, d, f, g, h, j, k, l, m, n, p, q, r, s, t, v, w, x, y (y can be a vowel or a consonant), and z.

Blends: Two or three consonants next to each other each of which make a sound, such as fl, pr, spr, st, str, and tr. The letter x is considered a blend because it makes the sound /ks/. The letters qu make the sound /kw/ and are also considered a blend.

Digraphs: Two consonants next to each other that make only one sound. The letters ch, sh, th, wh, and ng are digraphs.

Vowels: Sounds, phonemes, which are NOT blocked when pronounced. The vowels are a, e, i, o, u, and sometimes y.

Short Vowels: /ă/ as in apple, /ĕ/ as in elephant or Ed, /ĭ/ as in igloo or itch, /ŏ/ as in octopus, and /ŭ/ as in umbrella or up.

CK Rule: The sound of /k/ can be spelled with c, k, or ck. After a short vowel, the /k/ sound is spelled with a ck.

Floss Rule: The /f/ sound can be spelled with f or ff; the /l/ sound can be spelled with l or ll; the /s/ sound can be spelled with s or ss, and the /z/ sound can be spelled with and s, z or zz. After a short vowel /f/ is spelled ff, /s/ is spelled ss, /l/ is spelled ll, and /z/ is spelled zz. Those two letters (ff, ll, ss, zz) still only make one sound.

Use of s: s is added to nouns and verbs for syntax.

Use of 's: 's is used to indicate possession.

Use of es: To form a plural of a noun, usually add s. However, when a noun ends with s, x, z, ch, or sh, form the plural by adding es.

Silent e Rule: When an e is at the end of a word, it often causes the previous vowel to become long. For example, at becomes ate, mad becomes made, rid becomes ride, and us becomes use. Words such as Mae, lie, doe, and blue can also be considered to be following the Silent e Rule even though there is no consonant between the vowel and the final "silent" e.

Compound Words: Compound Words: A compound word is two or more words, each of which could stand alone, but, also, could be joined together, forming a new word often with a new meaning. Examples of compound words are landslide, milkman, and pancake. Words such as across, alike, and along are also classified as compound words because the **a** (short u (/ŭ/ as in umbrella /ŭ/ or up /ŭ/) as in "Once upon **a** time" can stand alone as a single word, but it can also be joined with cross (across), like (alike), and long (along) to form a compound word. A compound word can be written as a single word (handmade) or as a hyphenated word (first-class).

Vowel Reference Card: The Vowel Reference Card is composed of the most COMMON vowel sounds as found in <u>Remedial Training for Children with Specific Disability in Reading, Spelling, and Penmanship</u> by Anna Gillingham and Bessie W. Stillman, Seventh Edition, Copyright 1960. It does NOT include all the possible ways to say and/or spell those sounds in English.

ABOUT THE AUTHOR/ILLUSTRATOR

Carolyn Torres (c.torres@laschools.net), M.Ed., and teacher of 27 years (14 in various grades in elementary, 12 in middle school, and 1 in high school) has remained a National Board-Certified Teacher since 1995 when National Board Certification began. She is currently working on her doctorate while teaching 3rd grade for Los Alamos Public Schools, where she has been an active mentor, teacher, and math coach. She was a national NSF Coalition of Essential Schools Fellow, a Master Teacher for the New Mexico Electronic Bridge Project, and she co-authored a 3rd grade CCSS-based online curriculum for Lincoln Learning Solutions. Carolyn Torres was the 2014 New Mexico State Teacher of the Year and a 2017 National STEM Fellow.

Nicholas Torres MEd, has over 20 years of experience in executive management. He built and led one of the largest and most nationally recognized human services organizations, founded and governed two charter schools, founded a nonprofit focused on scaling high impact social enterprises including school-based health centers and high school/college access and completion pipelines, and founded a social sector consulting organization. Currently, he is president of social innovations partners which publishes the social innovations journal and facilitates the social innovations institute & lab. He serves as adjunct faculty at University of Pennsylvania. He started parent reading coach with his colleagues because he believes parents and caregivers are the primary vehicles toward quality education and should have the educational tools and knowledge to educate their children.

Answer Key

The Tall Oak Tree
1. **c) at night, in the moonlight**
2. **c) at daylight, at sunup**
3. **b) the red hawk**
4. **b) the gray crane and the brown and green wood duck**
5. **a) the red and gold finch**

The Real Girl
1. Doc wants to make a **b) doll** into a **b) real girl**.
2. The skull has two **c) ears**, two blue **c) eyes**, a **c) nose**, and a **c) mouth** with lips and teeth.
3. **a) the lungs**
4. The long arms give **c) joy**. The short forearms with hands can **c) wave**. The **c) feet** can run.
5. **c) Doc did use her wishbone and said, "ZAP!"**

The Farm
6. **a) the cat and the pup**
7. **c) names**
8. **b) They cluck**.
9. **b) the cat and a duck**
10. The sheepdog **b) rounds up** the sheep and takes good **b) care** of them.

The Seeds
1. **b) seeds**
2. **a) popcorn seeds**
3. Once the seeds did sprout, the small boy left **c) one** plant in each hole.
4. The seeds need **c) rain** and **c) sunshine** to sprout and grow.
5. **c) the small boy**
6. "We will heat the **a) popcorn** in **a) hot oil** in a pan on the **a) stove**.

What is in the Lake?
1. **c) trout, goldfish, catfish**
2. **a) the whale, the shark, and toads**
3. **b) crabs**
4. **a) the toad**
5. **a) the toad**

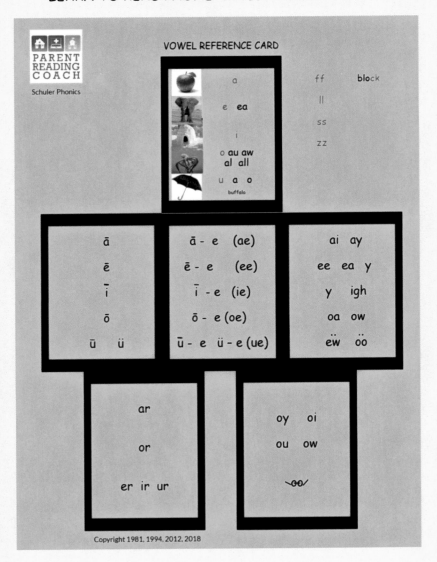

Made in the USA
Middletown, DE
19 October 2022